NEW IDEAS FOR NEEDLEPOINTERS

NEW IDEAS FOR NEEDLEPOINTERS

MARION BROOME PAKULA

CROWN PUBLISHERS, INC.
NEW YORK

To my mother

Inquiries should be addressed to Crown Publishers, Inc., One Park Avenue, New York, N.Y. 10016.

*Printed in the United States of America
Published simultaneously in Canada by
General Publishing Company Limited*

Designed by Ruth Smerechniak

Library of Congress Cataloging in Publication Data

Pakula, Marion Broome.
New ideas for needlepointers.

Includes index.
1. Canvas embroidery—Patterns.   I. Title.
TT778.C3P345   746.4'4   75-37799
ISBN 0-517-52473-2
ISBN 0-517-52474-0 pbk.

Contents

ACKNOWLEDGMENTS

Many thanks to all my friends who labored to finish their pieces so that they could be included in this book: Jack Shaffer of Huntington, N.Y.; Rhoda Goldberg of Dix Hills, N.Y.; Lucille Goldman of East Williston, N.Y.; Lois Nalevaiko of Port Jefferson, N.Y.; Eleanor Frank of Commack, N.Y.; Mayjean Adler of The Point, Glen Head, N.Y.; Barbara Corin of Glen Cove, N.Y.; and Norma Levy of Huntington, N.Y. Special thanks to Nedda Balter of Seaford, N.Y., who did all the diagrams. As always, I am grateful to Eleanor Frank for her expert finishing of all the pillows and most of the other items as well. And finally, thanks to all the babies for whom the birth-date pillows were made, for they stretched my mind and generated all of Idea 4.

Introduction

In the course of an assignment featuring needlepoint designs with the masculine touch, many ideas came to me. I thought in terms of bold designs, many geometrical in feeling, and one by one the designs took shape. When I looked back at them, I found that they all had some connection with numbers. Later I realized that they could be used by women as well as men, with a simple change in color.

I like personalized needlepoint, and so do many of my clients. Adults and children are alike in that they are both pleased in seeing their names in print (or in needlepoint!). So I developed an interest in unusual alphabets. This led to the All-Over Initial pattern as one use for these letters. Big letters can be used for a contemporary design with real impact. Such a name can become the entire design, as on a tennis racquet cover, a briefcase, or a handbag.

Much of the time we stitch in wool. Translating woven wool fabric designs into needlepoint was fun. Just try the houndstooth patterns and you'll see for yourself!

Of course, birthdays are always with us, and lots of people like to make needlepoint birthday gifts. With my fascination for numbers, it was an easy step to make number patterns from the numbers in a birth date (or any other date). The delighted response from those whose birthdays were so immortalized was all I needed to develop more designs based on birth dates. Now we have six different designs with several variations based on a date.

I hope that you will have as much fun with these new ideas as I had developing them. If the reaction I have already seen is any criterion, there will be many happy needlepointers experimenting on graph paper, *thinking* needlepointers who plan individual designs and enjoy doing it.

mbp
August 11, 1975

All-Over Initial

Personalized pieces have great appeal, and this new idea is as personal as can be. Prominent designers and businesses have used their own initials to create a status symbol, spreading them over scarves, fabric, and luggage. Now you can create your own, using the All-Over initial pattern.

The entire article is made up of an initial (or several) arranged within boxes in a cascading diagonal design. As shown in Diagram 1, there is a border of one row of stitches around the letter. Making use of the box allows for a multicolored design—one for the letter, one for the box, and one for the background. It is usually easier to stitch the letters and the surrounding box in a simple diagonal stitch, but you may use your imagination for the background with fancy stitches or a repeating pattern for added interest. One repeating background is shown on the checkbook cover.

On the other hand, the box can be used only as a guide to place the letter, and then the box lines can be ignored when stitching. Just fill the background to the edge of the letter, as in the "FS" pillow and "P" magazine rack.

11

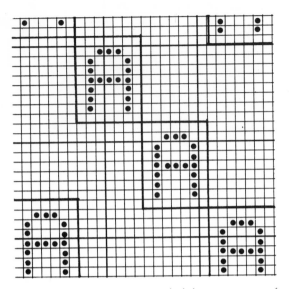

Diagram 1. Letter surrounded by one row of stitches to form a box

Pillow made by Mrs. Sol Broome of New York City with the initials FS in three colors on a neutral background.

Diagonal box patterns are given for four different sizes, coinciding with some of the alphabets designed by the author. A small personal article such as the checkbook cover calls for a small letter and box. But you would use a larger letter and box for a larger piece such as a floor pillow, footstool, or hooked rug.

Magazine rack sling. The small black letter is from the DMC alphabet shown on pages 44–45. It was enlarged to form the overlay in the same style by multiplying the number of stitches by four in each direction. Thus, each single stitch in the original letter became a 4-stitch-by-4-stitch square. Any design can be similarly enlarged with the same method, multiplying a single stitch by any number to achieve the desired size.

Diagram 2. 7-stitch-by-9-stitch box design

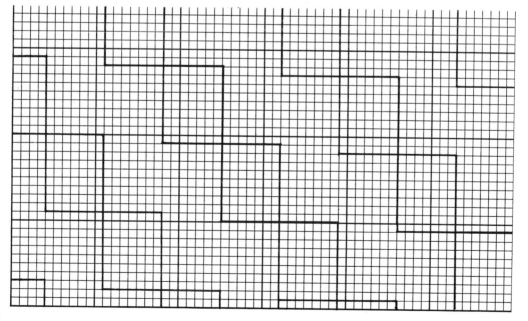

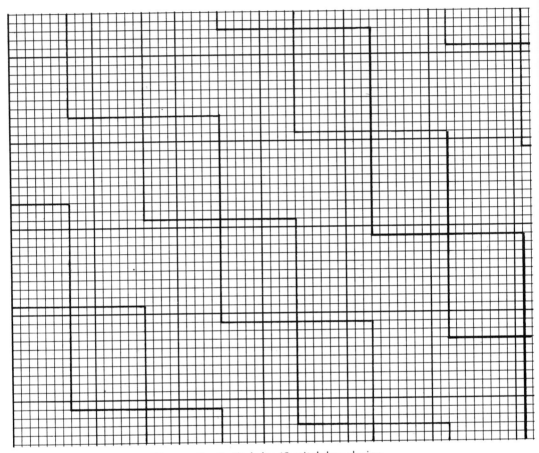

Diagram 3.   9-stitch-by-12-stitch box design

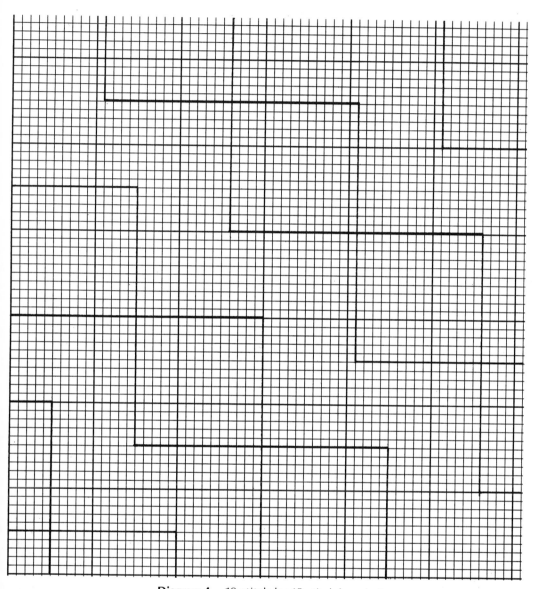

Diagram 4.   19-stitch-by-15-stitch box design

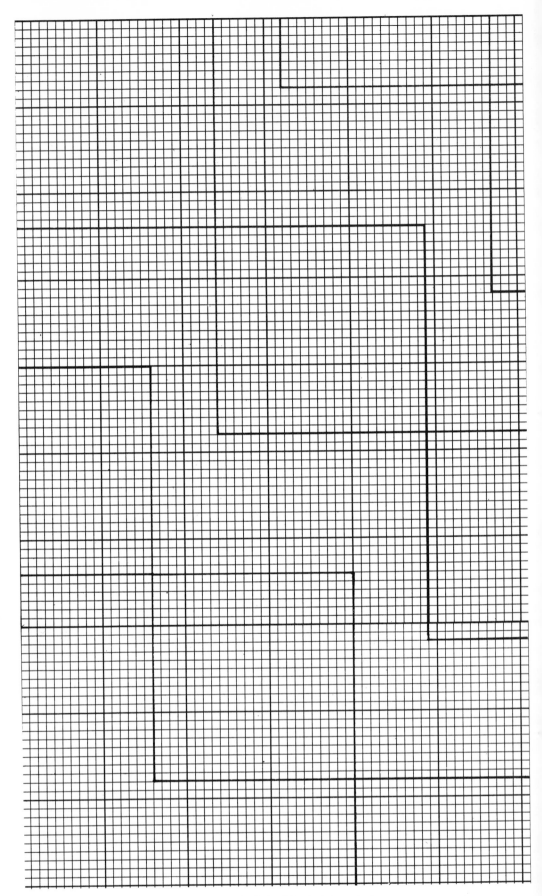

Diagram 5. 24-stitch-by-24-stitch box design

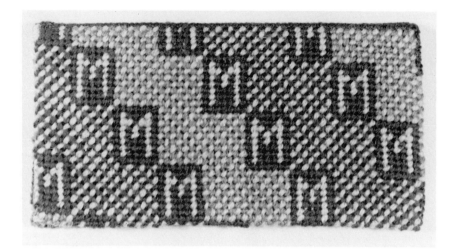

Checkbook cover in two shades of green, using the smallest letter. Every other stitch in alternating colors was used for part of the background.

The "E" case uses two shades of one color; the "S" case uses two colors with white. Eyeglass cases made by Eleanor Frank of Commack, N.Y.

Some of the alphabets in the next chapter are larger, and you can make up your own box design according to the size of the letter you use. Allow two or more rows of stitches all around the letter and make the box lines. Attach the lower right corner of one box to the upper left corner of the next box below it. Use the box designs shown as a guide for making up your own. Pencil in a letter on the graph paper provided at the back of the book, then draw straight lines around it to make the proper box size. Remember that every square on the graph paper represents one stitch on your canvas, and the area covered by the design will depend on the size mesh you are using.

Footstool cover executed in the All-Over Initial pattern by Mayjean Adler of The Point, Glen Head, N.Y., from a charted design drawn by the author.

Alphabets, New and Old

If you're like many other needlepointers, you are always searching for new letter styles. Since every needlepointer is an artist, letters are needed to sign a piece in the corner. The size required will vary, depending on the design of the piece. Sometimes there isn't much room, but you still want to stitch your initials and maybe the date. Then again, to make a bold statement with letters, as in the All-Over Initial pattern, you will need letters that are quite large.

Ten different letter styles are given, from the smallest and simplest that covers only 7 stitches high by 5 stitches wide, to the largest that covers 23 stitches high by 24 stitches wide. Although all charts were drawn on 10-squares-to-the-inch graph paper, the area of canvas covered will vary, depending on the mesh size.

Through the kind permission of the DMC Corporation, some alphabets from their library of old letters are reproduced here, along with alphabets created by the author.

Tennis visor stitched on 12 mesh canvas. The V is from author's alphabet on pages 24–26. Sculpture courtesy of Valerie Malkin of Westfield, N.J.

Diagram 6. Small capital letters and numbers covering 5 stitches wide by 7 stitches high

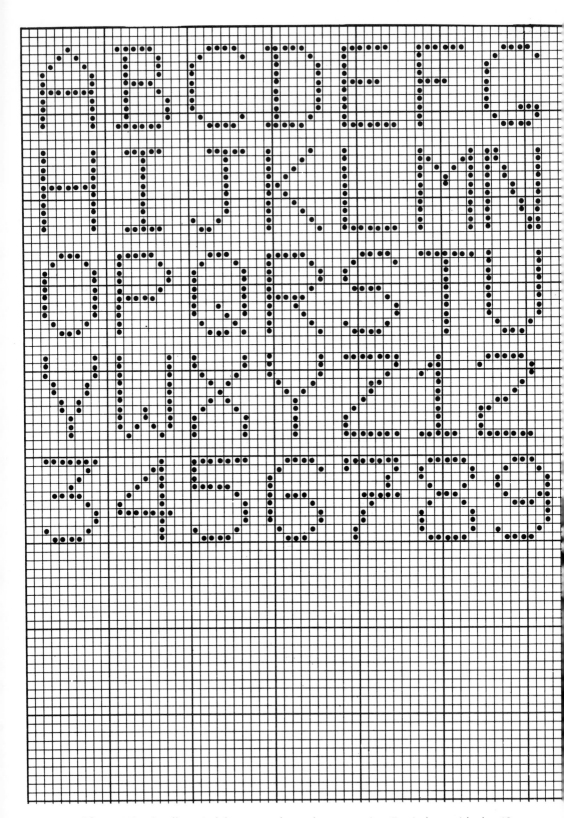

Diagram 7. Small capital letters and numbers covering 7 stitches wide by 10 stitches high

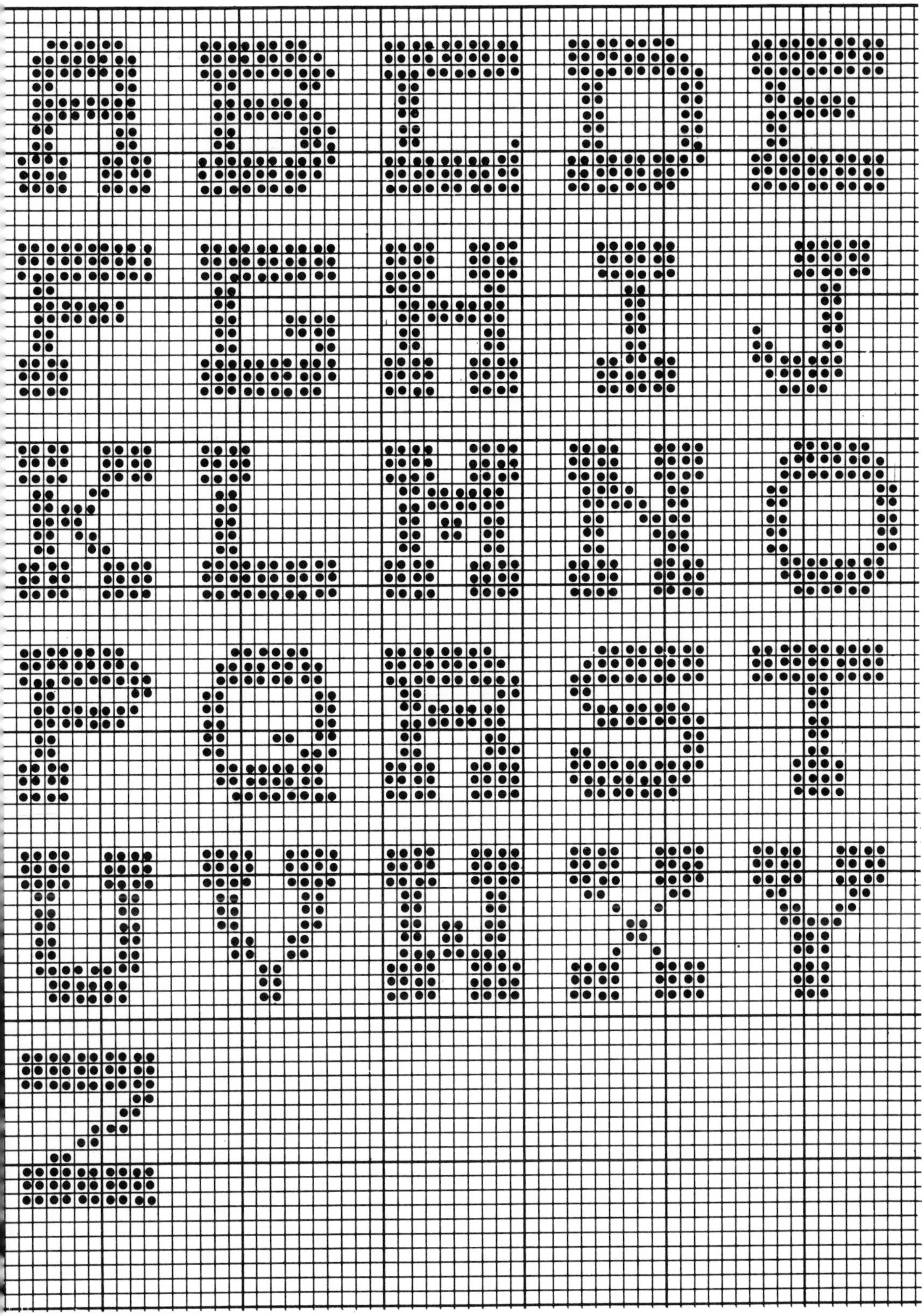

Diagram 8. Poster-style alphabet covering 10 stitches wide by 11 stitches high

9a

Diagrams 9a, 9b, 9c. Fat chunky letters and numbers covering 15–18 stitches wide by 17 stitches high

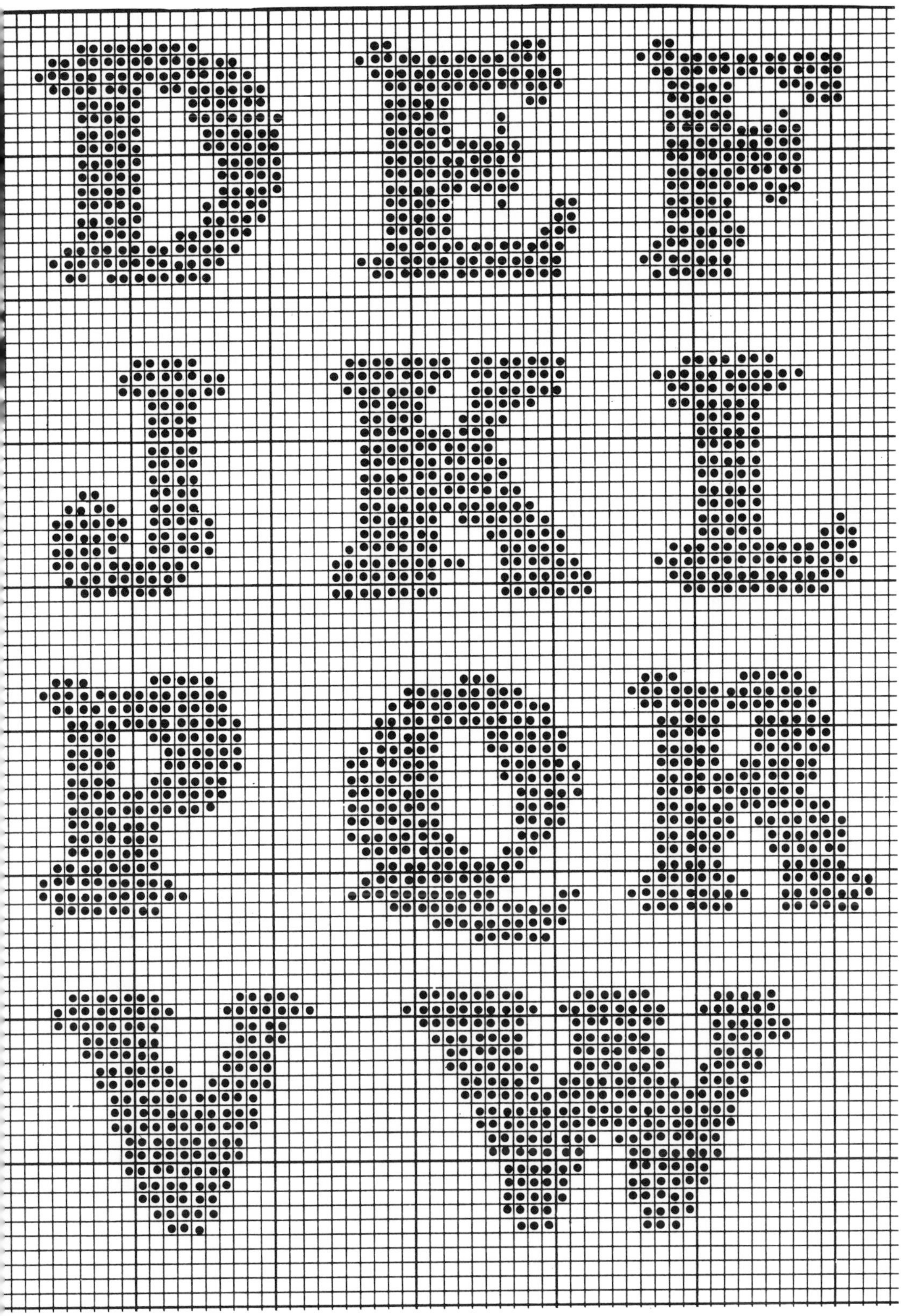

9b

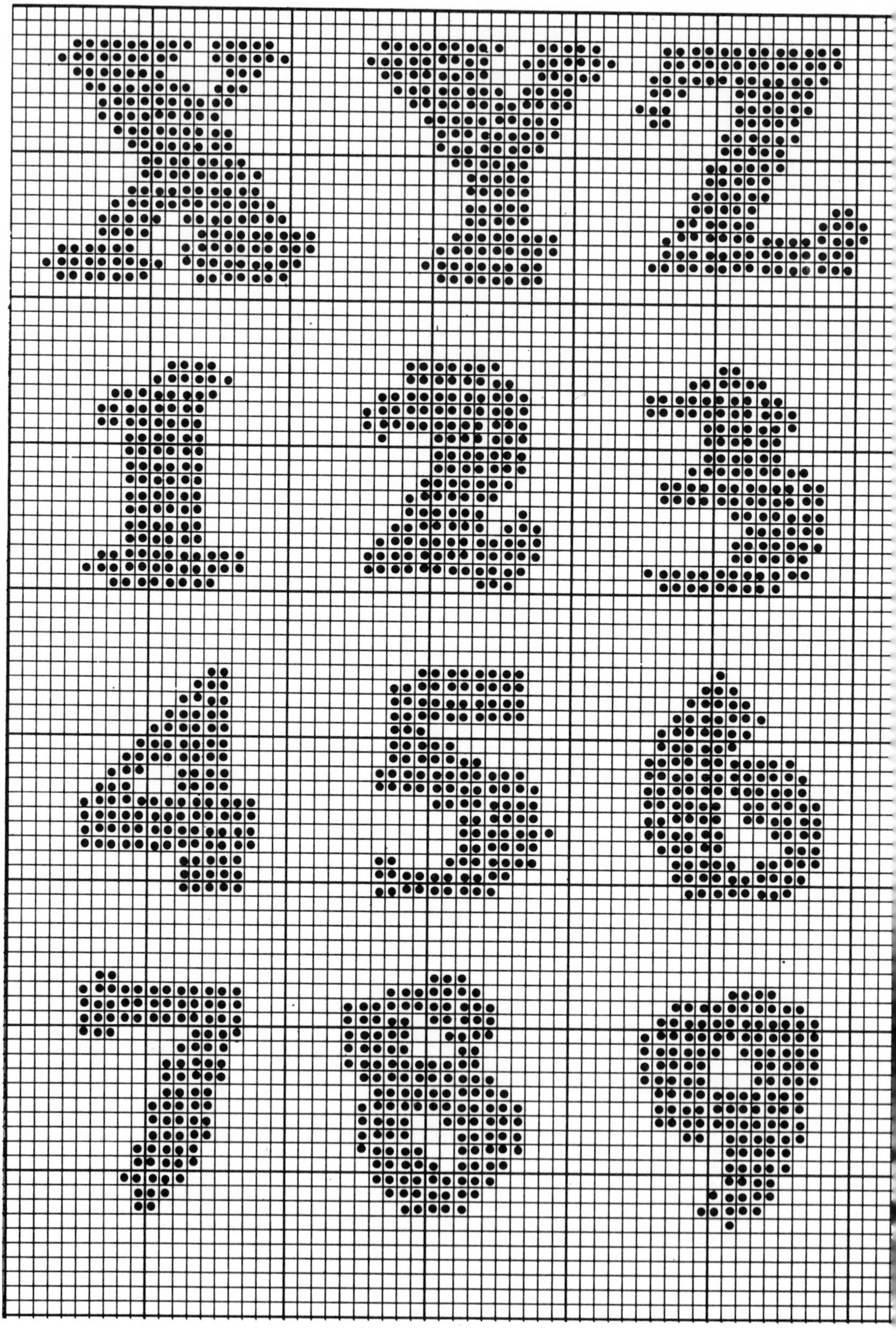

9c

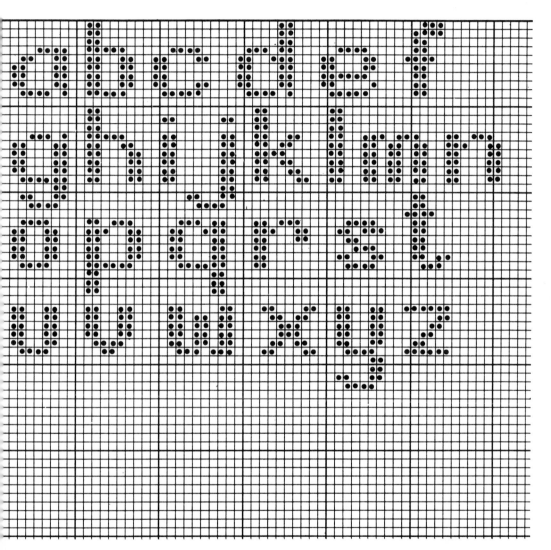

Diagram 10. Lowercase alphabet covering 6–8 stitches wide by 6–9 stitches high

Diagrams 11a, 11b, 11c, 11d, 11e, 11f.   Ornate lowercase letters and numbers

b

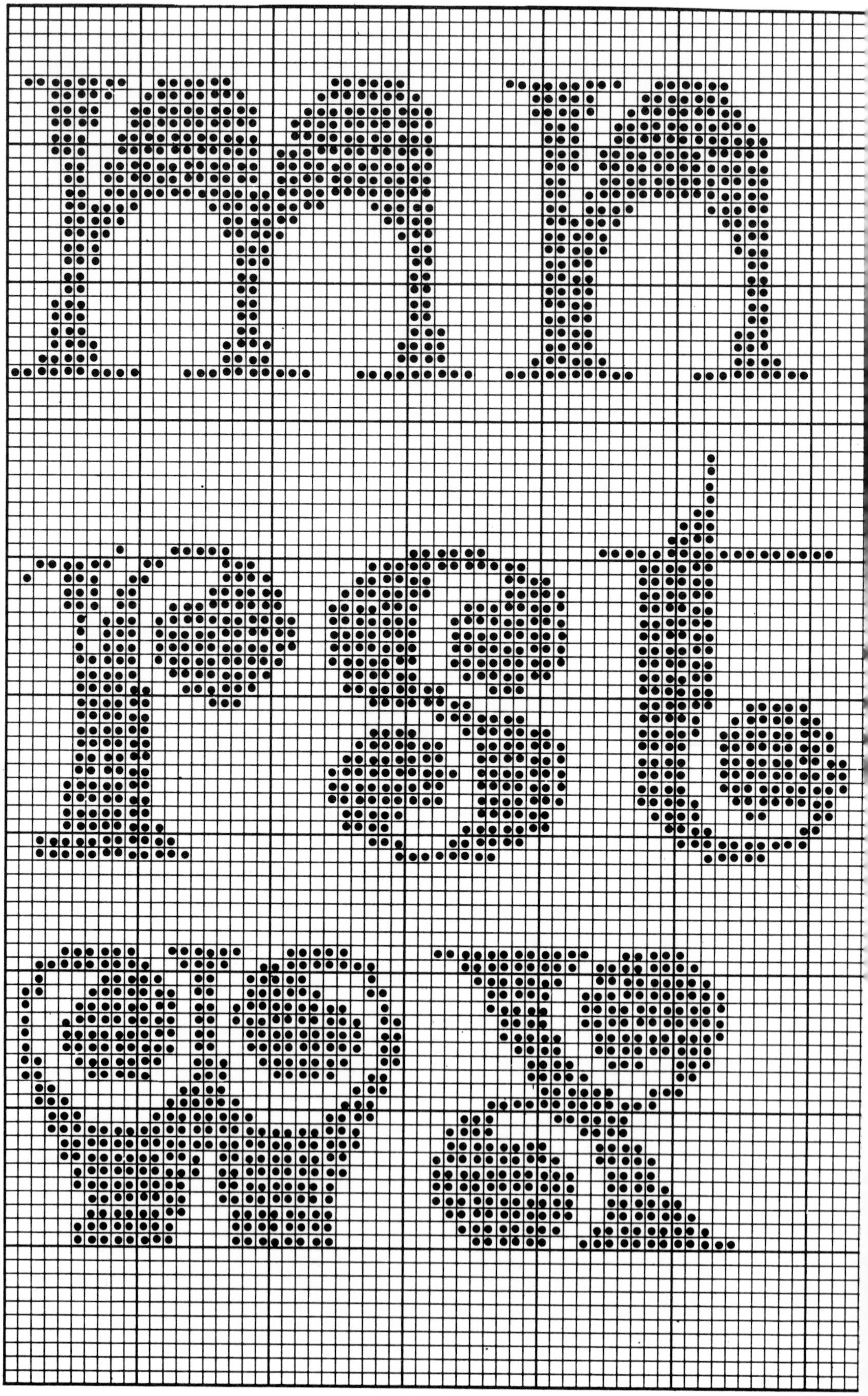

11c

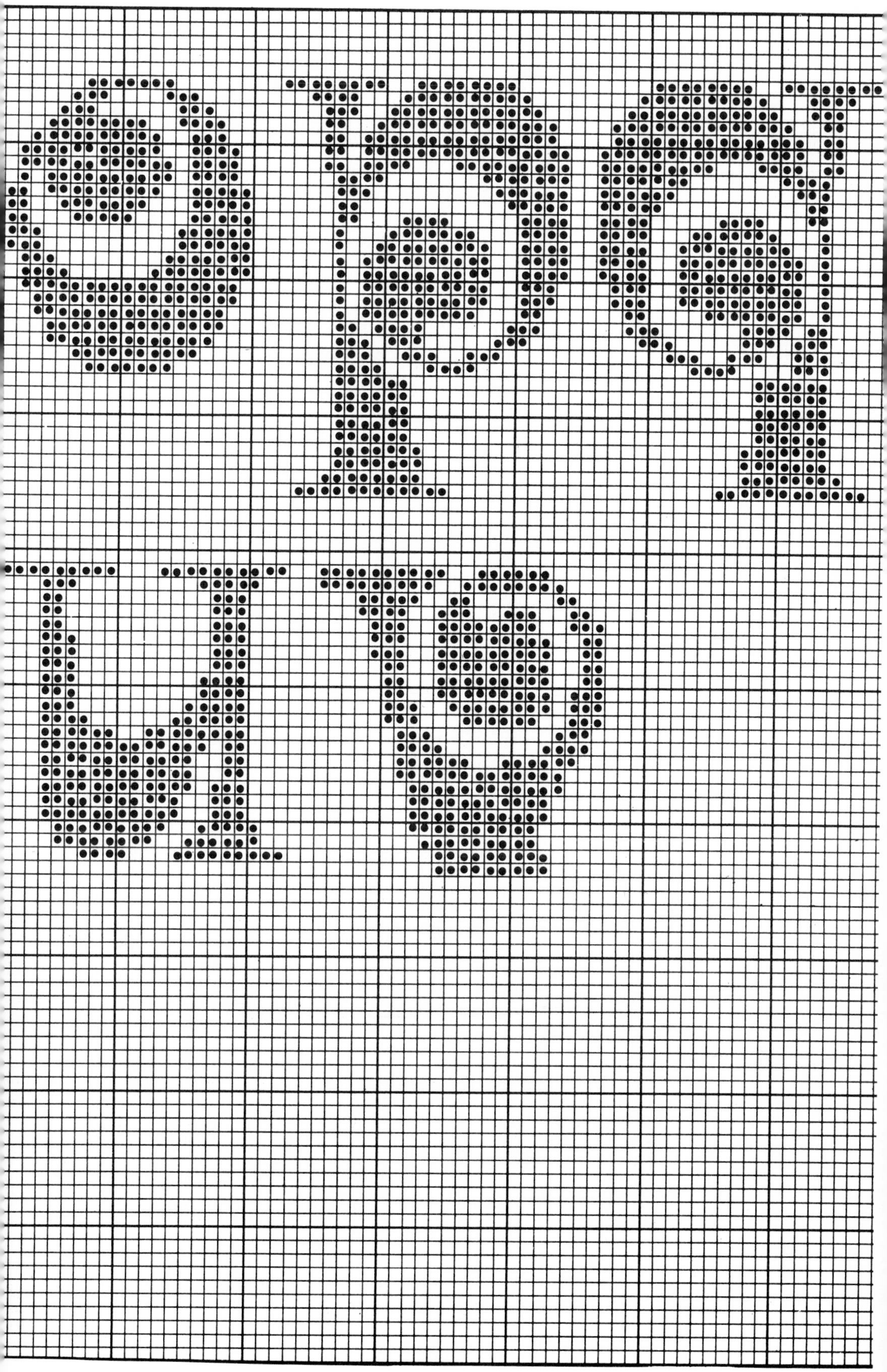

d

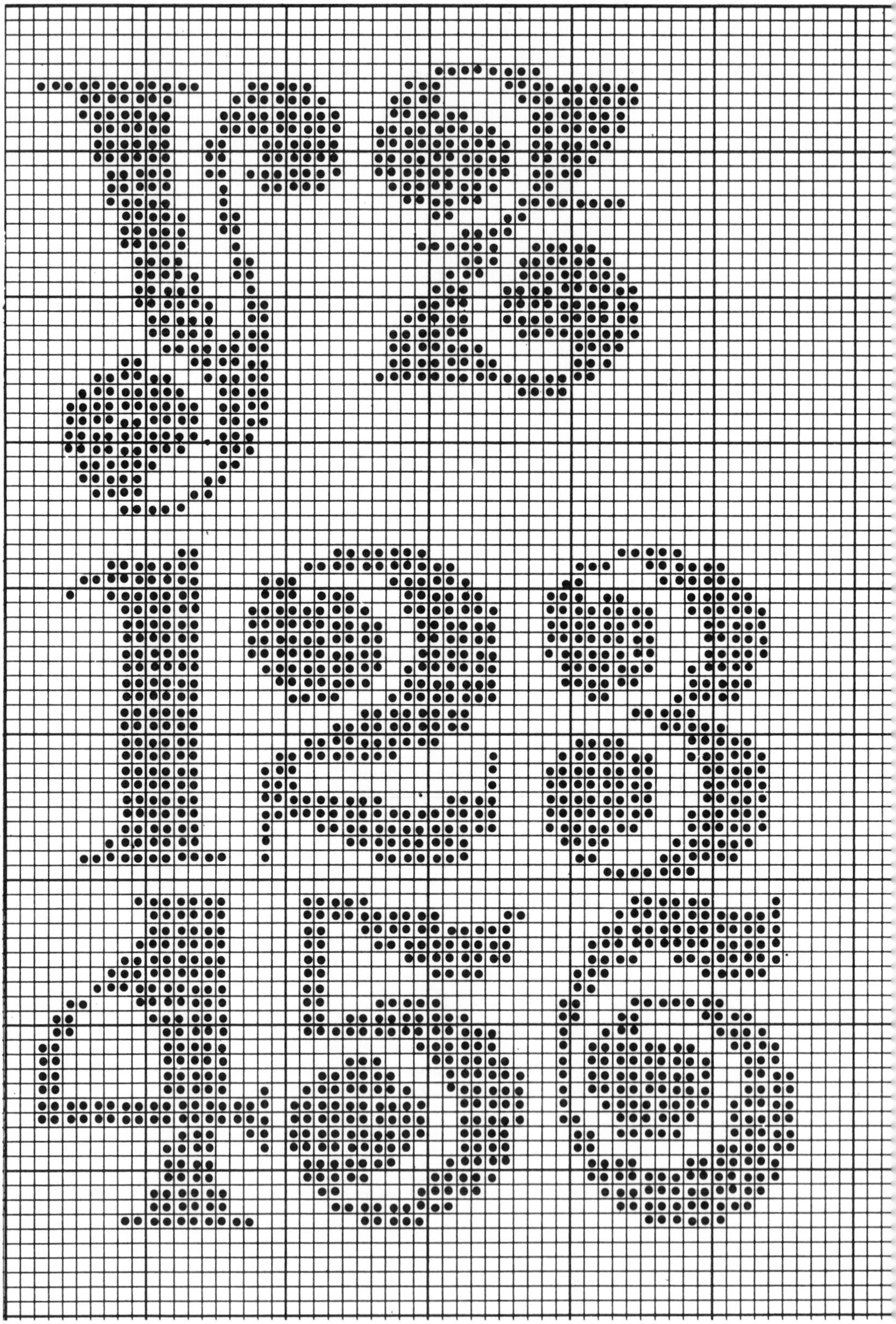

11e

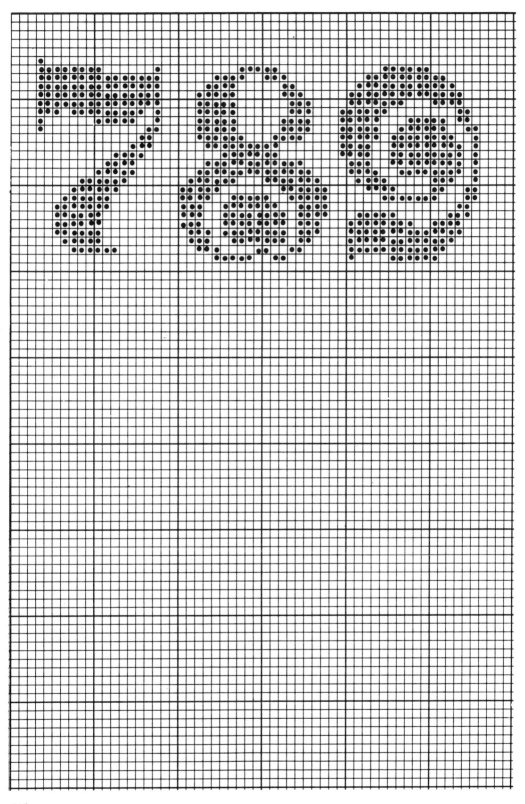

11f

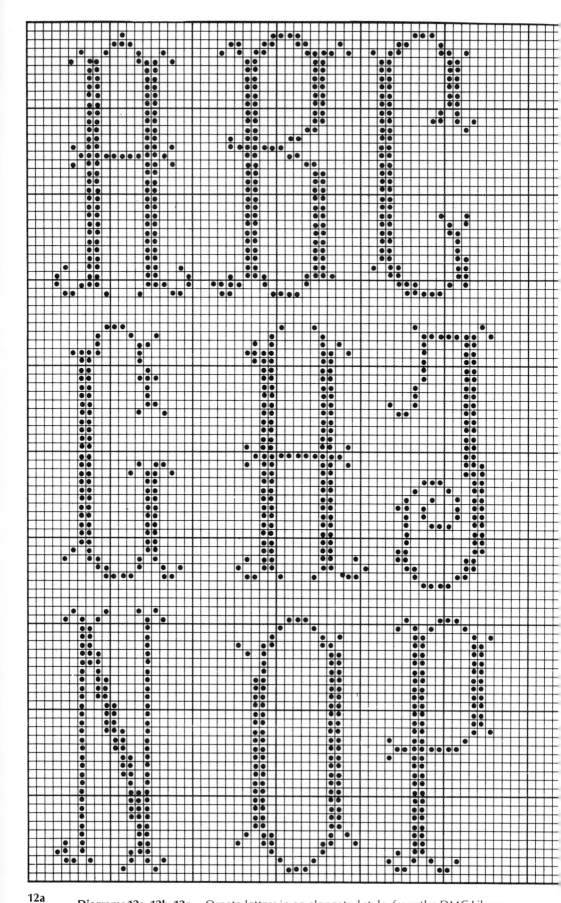

12a   **Diagrams 12a, 12b, 12c.**   Ornate letters in an elongated style, from the DMC Library

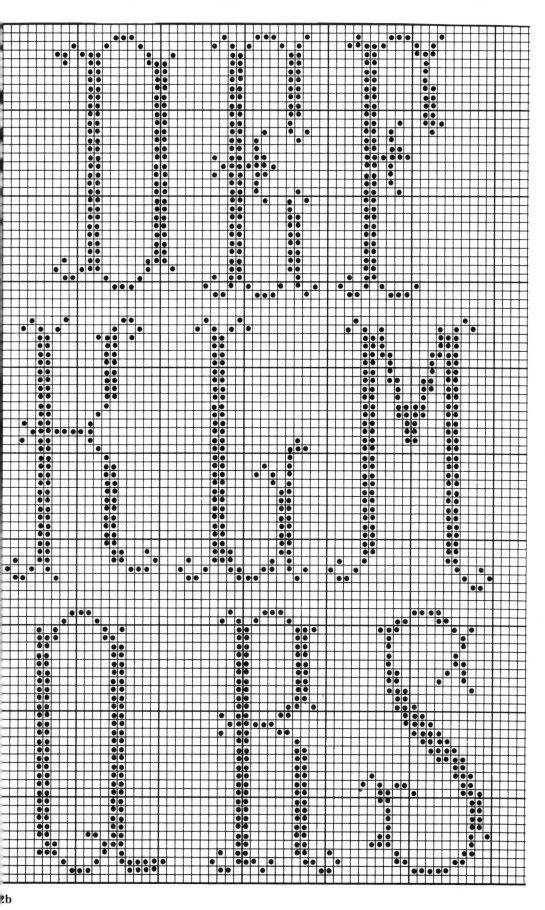

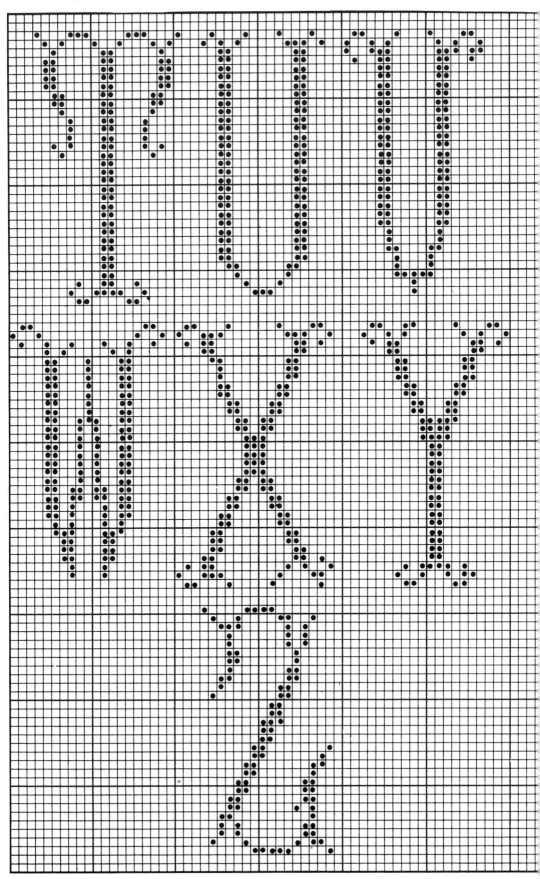

12c

Sampler made by the author in a modern DMC lettter, using two shades of red and two shades of green on a white basketweave ground. It was overlaid at the edges with a single strand of Persian yarn in cross-stitch.

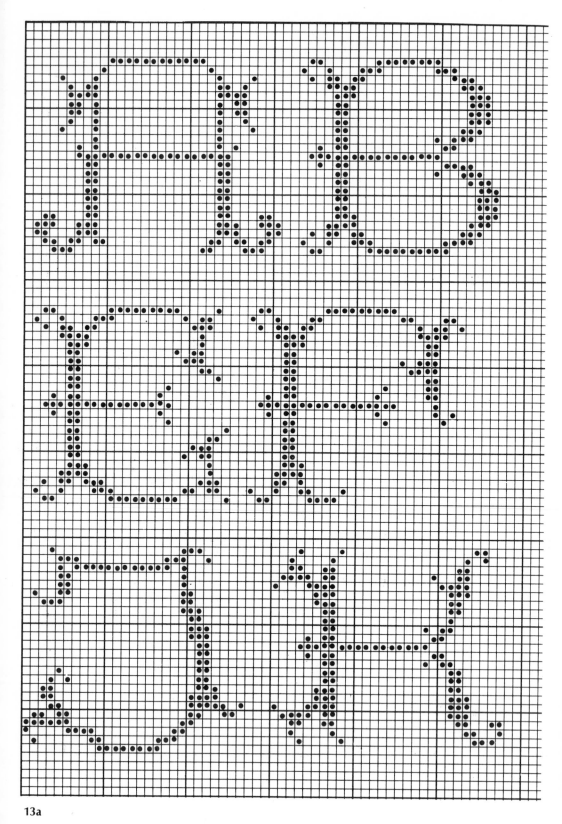

13a

Diagrams 13a, 13b, 13c, 13d, 13e. Ornate letters and numbers in a widened style, from the DMC Library

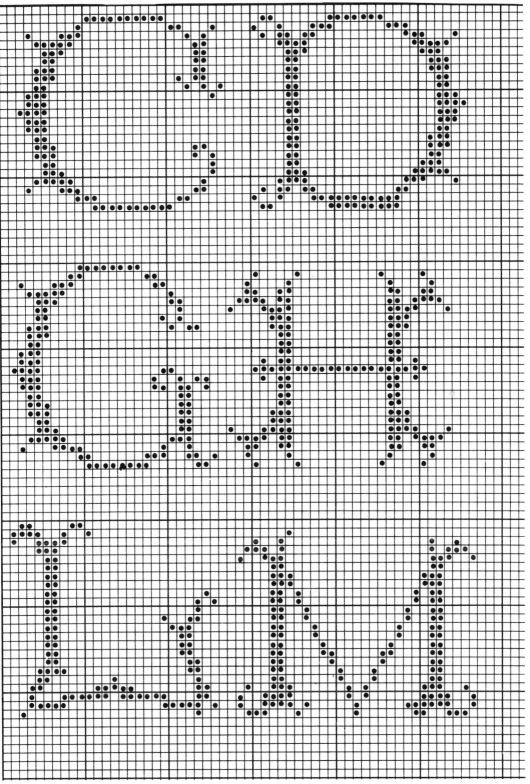

13b

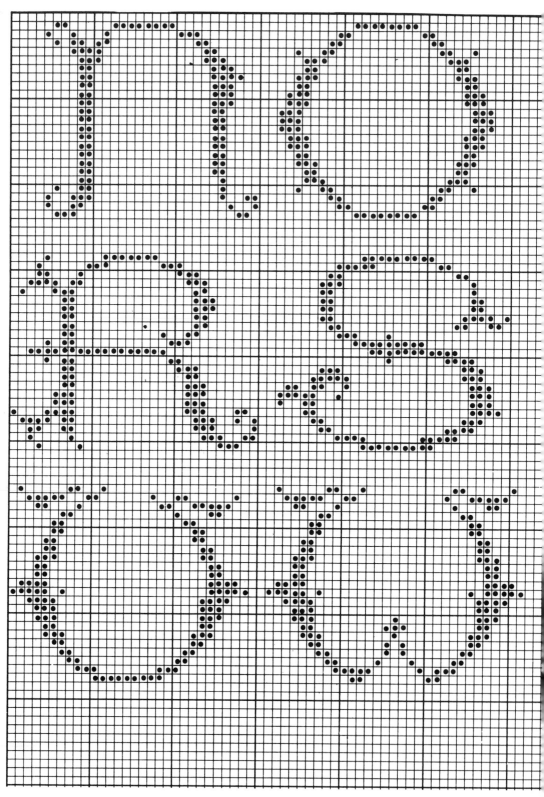

13c

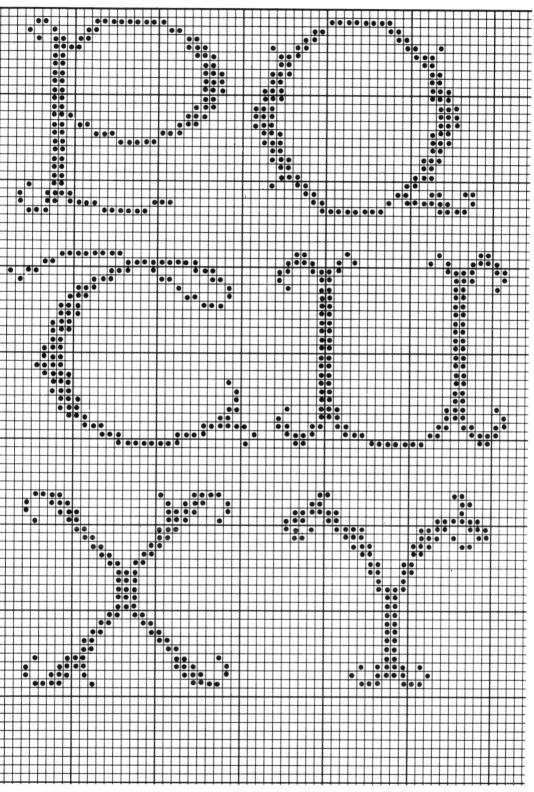

d

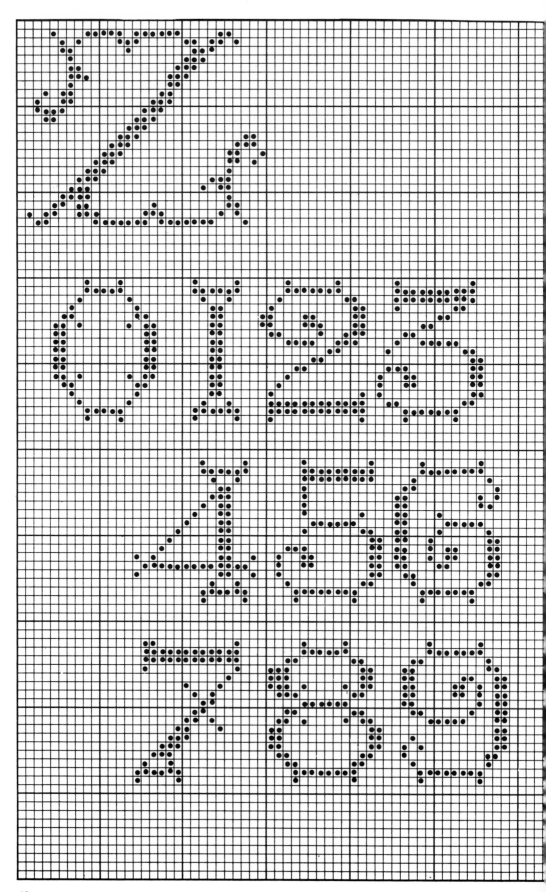

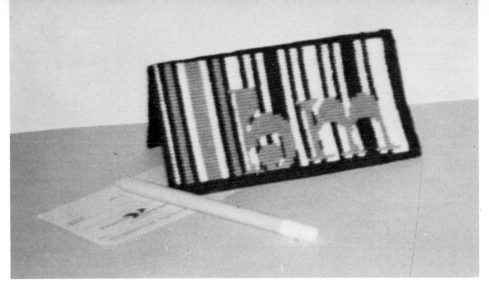

Checkbook cover using the letters from the author's ornate lower case alphabet on pages 28–32. The background stripe pattern is (center) 5A (navy blue), 2B (white), 2A, 2B, 2A, 4B, 2A, 2B, 2A, 2B, then repeat from 5A. On the left side of the design, pink was used instead of white for several sections to highlight the color of the letters.

ALTERING LETTERS

All of these letter styles may be altered to suit your own needs. To shorten a letter, simply eliminate one or more stitches in the vertical line of the letter. Be sure to do this on both sides when appropriate, as in an H or an M. To lengthen a letter, just add one or more stitches to both sides of the vertical lines. To make a letter narrower, eliminate one or more stitches on the horizontal lines of the letter, both top and bottom, as in a D or an E. To widen a letter, add one or more stitches to the horizontal lines.

The same style letter on a needlepointed hatband—a great way to turn an inexpensive straw hat into a showpiece. If you attach the hatband using Velcro dots, you can change the hatband to match any outfit!

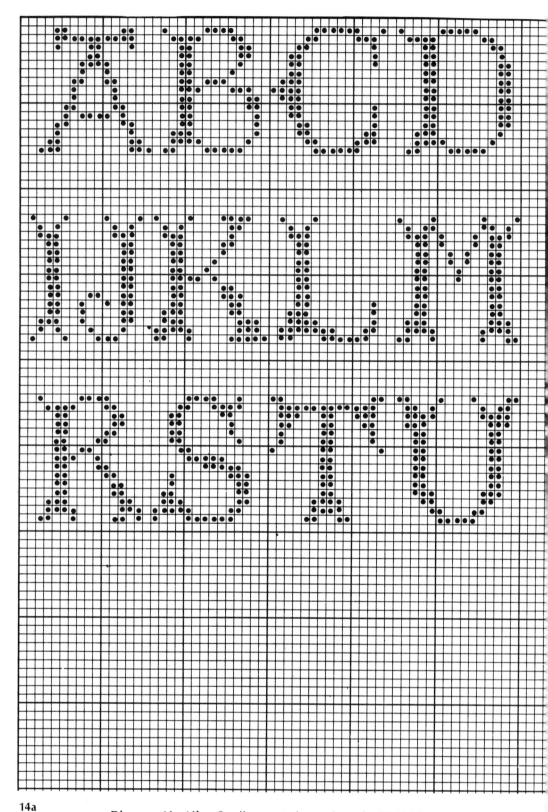

Diagrams 14a, 14b.   Smaller ornate letters from the DMC Library

b

Houndstooth Patterns

The houndstooth pattern has been a popular textile weave for centuries. It is used in men's and women's clothing as well as upholstery fabric and draperies. We even find it on luggage and plastic! When the houndstooth is translated into a needlepoint pattern, it can be executed in two ways. One is very small, and the other we call the "running" houndstooth.

SMALL HOUNDSTOOTH

The small houndstooth design can be done in two colors very easily, stitching directly from the chart as one would do with any other charted design, or using the two-row "every-other-stitch" as shown in Diagrams 24, 25, and 26. All you have to do is decide on your two colors, then stitch every other stitch for two rows of each color both horizontally and vertically. The houndstooth will appear like magic when the horizontal and vertical rows of the same color meet!

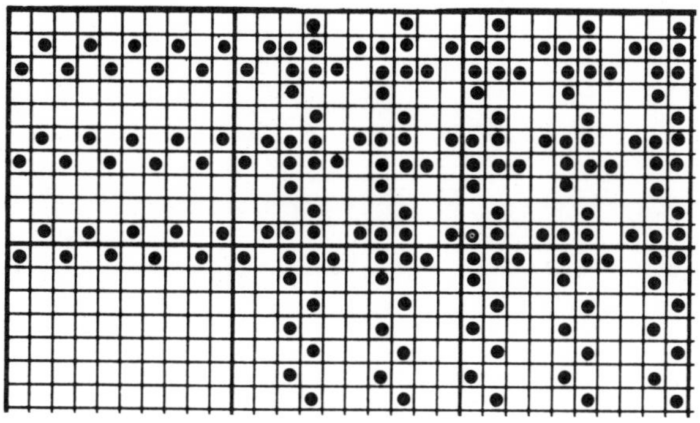

Diagram 15. Small houndstooth, basic size

Diagram 16. Small houndstooth, doubled

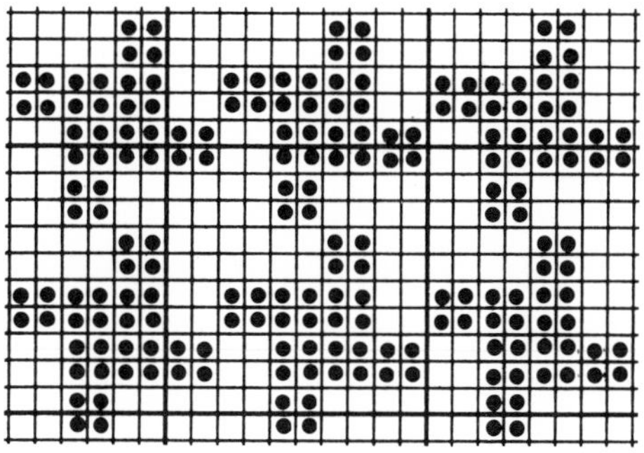

Diagram 17. Small houndstooth, tripled

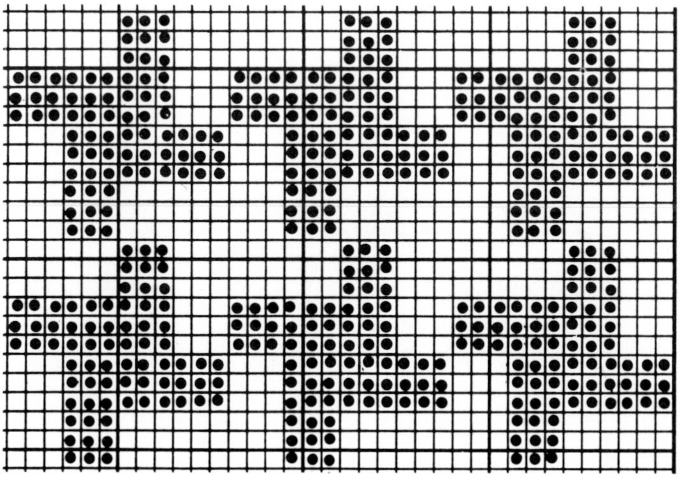

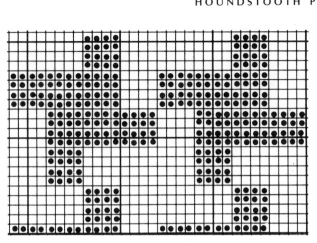

Diagram 18.   Small houndstooth, four times basic size

Diagram 19.   Small houndstooth, five times basic size

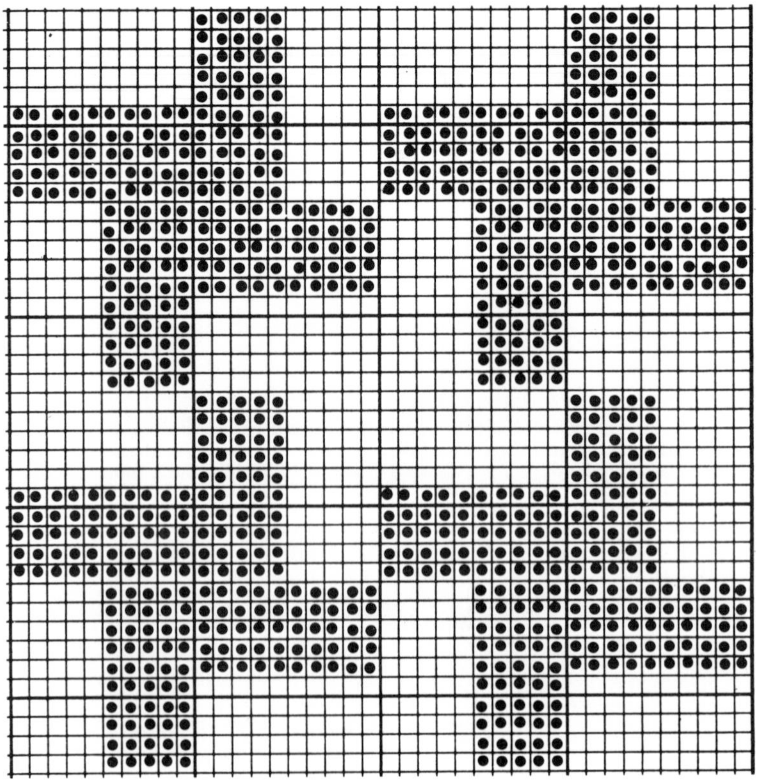

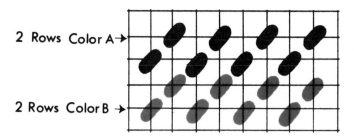

2 Rows Color A →

2 Rows Color B →

Diagram 20. Every other stitch, horizontal, for two rows of each color

Color B   Color A

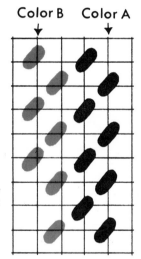

Diagram 21. Every other stitch, vertical, for two rows of each color

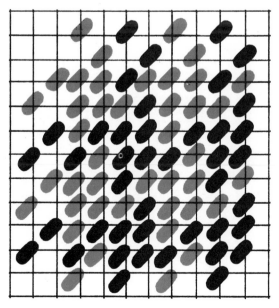

Diagram 22. Combined horizontal and vertical rows, creating the small houndstooth pattern

Color plays a large part in the effectiveness of the small houndstooth pattern. The contrast between light and dark (or complementary) colors defines the pattern. If you use shades of the same color, you will create an entirely different look, even though the two-row every-other-stitch method is used. You will see that the houndstooth fades away and you are left with a soft tweed pattern.

Paperback book cover/carrier in the small houndstooth design using three colors. Notice that in this one the lettering "SUSIE'S BOOK" was placed on the binding.

Pincushion made by Barbara Corin of Glen Cove, N.Y. The bottom and sides were stitched in stripes on plastic canvas, and the top was done on 14 mesh canvas using both the smallest houndstooth and the same design doubled.

A soft tweedy effect is achieved with this two-color small houndstooth design through the choice of colors of the same depth.

A lady's keycase using the small houndstooth combined with stripes. When finished, the middle section forms the back, and the side sections fold over each other and are closed with a heavy snap.

Keytag in the smallest houndstooth design stitched on 14 mesh canvas by Rhoda Goldberg. The letter is from the alphabet on pages 24–26.

Two-color small houndstooth applied to a telephone on 12 mesh canvas, and a notebook cover on 14 mesh canvas, both stitched using a single strand of ordinary sport yarn (commonly used for knitting), to achieve a neat, flat look. Notebook cover made by Rhoda Goldberg of Dix Hills, N.Y. The Accent telephone from the Design Line of the New York Telephone Company was used with their permission. The letters on both pieces are from the author's alphabet on pages 28–33.

A three-color pattern can have two sharp colors and one background color (white, beige, or a pale shade of one of the main colors). An interesting pattern can also be made using a very dark background (dark blue, dark green, brown, or black) or a neutral background (gray or beige) with two very bright colors, such as bright red, orange, yellow, electric blue, or bright green.

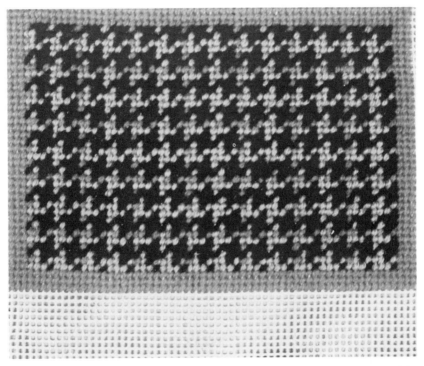

Three-color small houndstooth. In this case, a single row of a third color is combined with the two-row pattern of the other two colors. The pattern is [2A, 2B, 2A, 1C] repeated over and over in both directions.

DEVELOPING
A HOUNDSTOOTH COLOR PATTERN

The evolution of a pattern using five colors is shown in the photographs for this project. Two shades of brown and two shades of pink were used with beige.

In the first attempt at combining these colors, shown in the first photograph, the houndstooth pattern loses its definition where the two shades of pink are placed adjacent to each other. Using the same colors with different emphasis, the pinks show up more in the second photograph, but the houndstooth is visible mostly when the brown is adjacent to the pink. In the next photograph of the series, the browns are emphasized with pink used only for contrast. The most effective placement for these colors is shown in the last photograph, where beige was placed between each of the four other colors.

Developing a Houndstooth Color Pattern

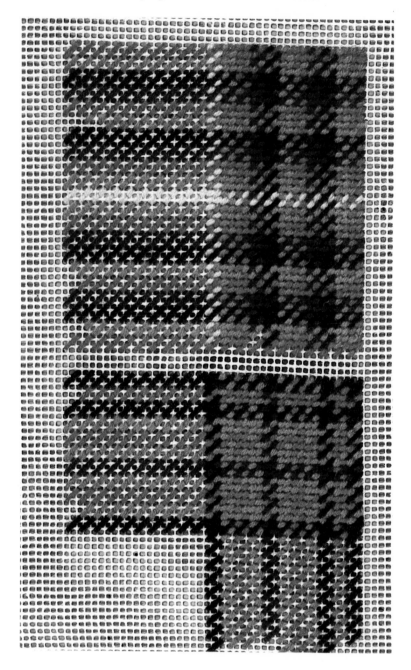

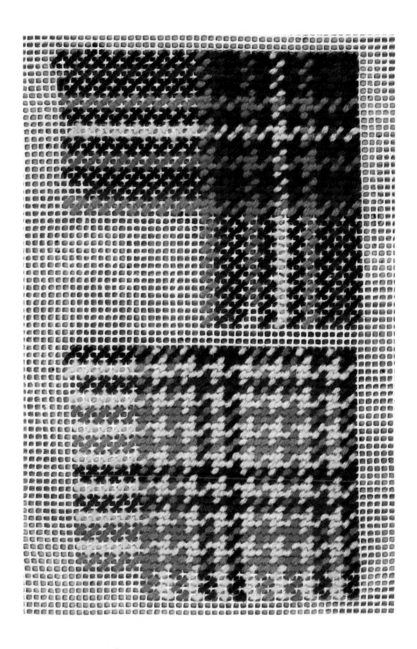

"RUNNING" HOUNDSTOOTH

With the "running" houndstooth there is more room for using fancy stitches in combination with the simple diagonal stitch, as shown in the paperback book cover/carrier. The design may be executed in two alternating colors, or you may insert a third color at random across the piece. When the expanded "running" houndstooth is used there is an opportunity for shading at the edges, as in the hooked wall hanging.

If you have any clothing made from a houndstooth patterned fabric, you can make a matching personal article like a purse, book carrier, or keycase. Also, if you have any furniture upholstered in a houndstooth fabric, you can make a matching needlepoint piece such as a footstool, picture frame, pillow, or even a hooked rug, using the charts as a guide.

Paperback book cover/carrier made in three colors in the largest "running" houndstooth design on 10 mesh canvas. A variation of the Scotch stitch was used in one section.

Diagram 23. "Running" houndstooth, basic size

Footstool covered in red and cream, the design combining the basic sizes of the "running" houndstooth with a border of the small houndstooth. The outside edge is every other basketweave stitch in alternating colors.

Man's eyeglass case in the basic "running" houndstooth in two colors.

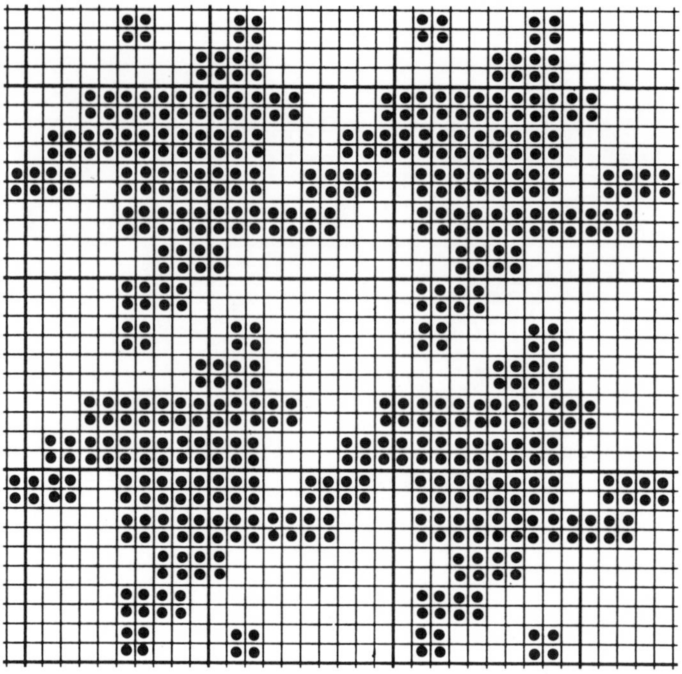

Diagram 24. "Running" houndstooth, doubled

Diagram 25. "Running" houndstooth, tripled

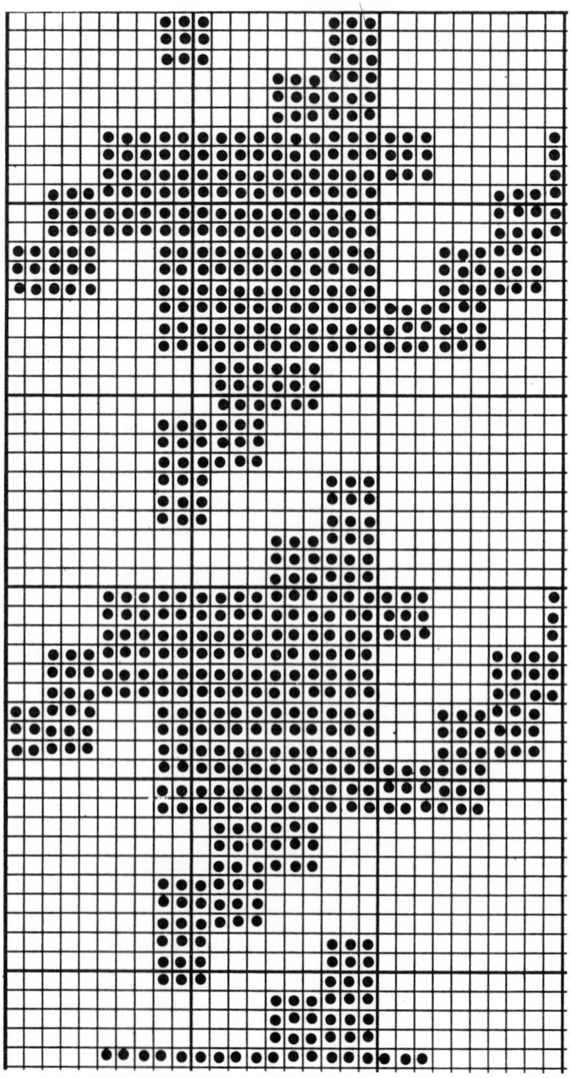

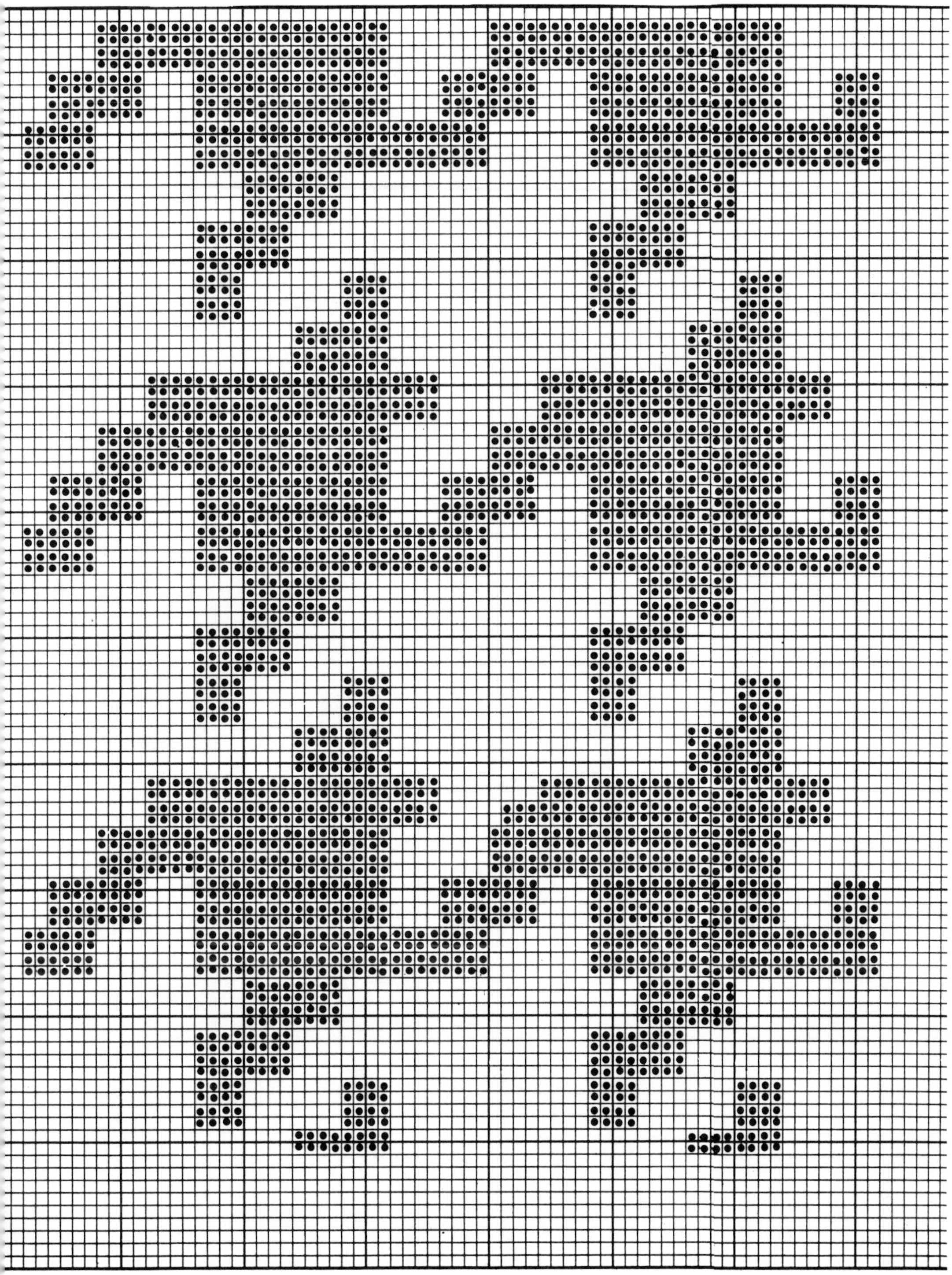

Diagram 26. "Running" houndstooth, four times basic size

Hooked wall hanging executed in brown, white, and gold by Mrs. Saul Goldman of East Williston, N.Y., in the largest size of the "running" houndstooth on 3½-to-the-inch rug canvas.

Sample of the basic "running" houndstooth design combined with stripes. This design has been used very effectively in red and black on a man's keycase/eyeglass case/wallet set.

Although women like the houndstooth, it is the men who really love it. The men and boys on your gift list will be pleasantly surprised to find that a needlepoint design can be made in a useful object which they will be proud to carry and use. The men in my family favor the keycase and eyeglass case in both houndstooth patterns.

Birth-Date Needlepoint

When the plaid stitch formula was first developed (in my book *Needlepoint Plaids*), it was suggested that readers develop plaid designs based on a telephone number or Social Security number. Since then, many pieces have been made based on a date, in response to requests for a unique baby gift. Much to my surprise, adults were jealous and wanted birth-date needlepoint for themselves! Many people also wanted to make gifts for wedding or anniversary celebrations using a special date to create the secret pattern.

HOW A DATE BECOMES A PATTERN

There are many different designs one can make using a pattern created from a simple number series such as a date. These numbers are used as a *count of the number of rows* to be stitched in a particular color. The patterns created from such a number series are different from each other, yet they all have one thing in common—the number of rows of each color is the same.

Symmetrical straight plaid baby pillow based on the date December 17, 1974.

Symmetrical straight plaid baby pillow based on the date October 9, 1974.

Symmetrical straight plaid baby pillow based on the date July 31, 1974.

You can make a vertical, horizontal, or diagonal stripe (either left- or right-directed). You can make a straight plaid or a diagonal plaid, sometimes called argyle. Any of these patterns can be symmetrical or repeating, and the repeating patterns may use the same color pattern or a different series of colors in each repeat. Each of these patterns is pleasing to the eye, easy to stitch, and suitable for application to many different articles.

To make a needlepoint number pattern from any date, take the month, day and year: XX XX XXXX. An example is November 9, 1974. The needle-point number pattern for this date would be 11-9-1-9-7-4. If you have a zero in your date, replace it with a 10. November 9, 1970 would have a pattern of 11-9-1-9-7-10.

If your "day" number is more than 20, you may want to split the number, separating it into two sections (23 could be 2-3). Otherwise, you will have a very large area covered by this one number, as in the FRANK pillow, which was based on July 31, 1974. Instead of 7-31-1-9-7-4, it could have been 7-3-1-1-9-7-4.

NUMBER PATTERNS

Number patterns tell you *how many* rows to stitch in a particular color. The sample patterns shown are given in both symmetrical and repeating versions. In a symmetrical design, the first number in the date (the month) is always the center, and each side is a mirror image of the other side. In a repeating pattern, however, you start at the outside edge of your piece with the "month" number. When you have stitched the last number of the year, just start again with the "month" number.

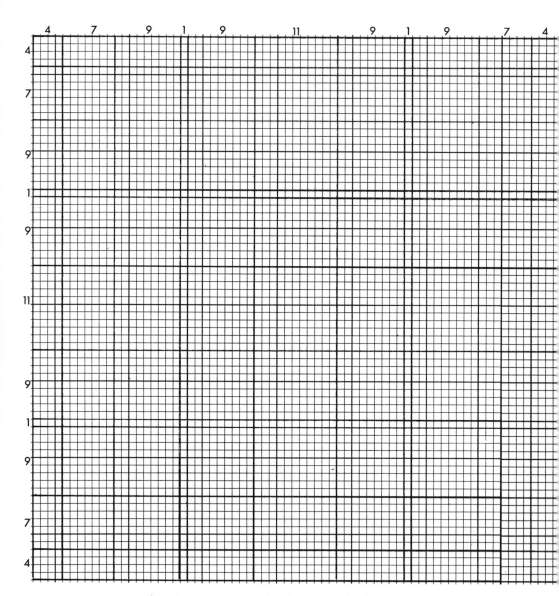

Diagram 27. Symmetrical straight plaid using the date November 9, 1974

Our basic example uses the birth date February 7, 1923. The symmetrical design has the month (February = 2) in the center.

$$3\ 2\ 9\ 1\ 7\ [2]\ 7\ 1\ 9\ 2\ 3$$

c
e
n
t
e
r

For a larger piece, the pattern is extended by reversing it on each side from the last number.

2 7 1 9 2 [3 2 9 1 7 [2] 7 1 9 2 3] 2 9 1 7 2
extension   basic   extension

The repeating pattern for this birth-date number pattern is simply

[2 7 1 9 2 3] [2 7 1 9 2 3] [2 7 1 9 2 3], etc.

COLOR PATTERNS

Color patterns tell you *what colors* to use in the different numbered sections. Symmetrical patterns use the same colors on both sides of the center. Repeating patterns may do the same thing, but here there is an opportunity for color variation if you like.

The basic color pattern of our example is A–B–C–B–A–C, with A = red, B = white, C = blue.

Number Pattern		Color Pattern
2	A	red
7	B	white
1	C	blue
9	B	white
2	A	red
3	C	blue

This color pattern can be repeated over and over, but you can also change the colors, still keeping the color pattern A–B–C–B–A–C.

STRIPES

The vertical and horizontal stripes are very simple. Just stitch the number of rows in your birth-date pattern in solid-colored sections, changing colors when you have finished the number of rows in a section. Depending on the intended use of your piece, you can use some fancy stitches in parts of your striped design for added interest.

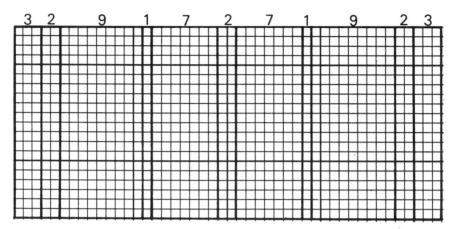

Diagram 28a.   Vertical stripe, symmetrical

Diagram 28b.   Horizontal stripe, symmetrical

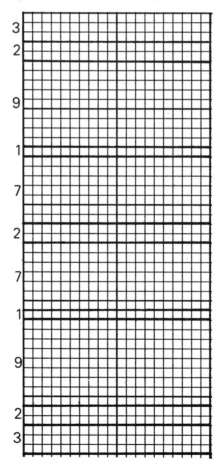

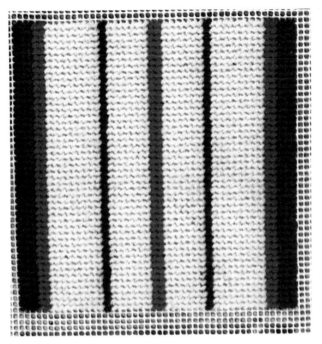

Symmetrical vertical stripe.

Symmetrical horizontal stripe.

Luggage rack straps made on 10 mesh canvas with repeating horizontal stripes based on the anniversary date January 11, 1948. Some fancy stitches were interspersed with basketweave for added texture. The letters are from the DMC alphabet on pages 34–36.

The diagonal striped design can be done either right-directed or left-directed. You will see that the left-directed stripe results in a sawtooth effect, while the right-directed stripe results in a straight line. Each of these diagonal-striped designs is best done with the basketweave stitch, since you can work much faster doing a single "up" or "down" row and you will save yarn in the long run. If you do the half-cross or tent stitch in single horizontal rows, you will be forced either to change your stitch or to turn your canvas to continue row by row. With the right-directed stripe, an entire section can be stitched at once with the basketweave stitch, moving down one row and one stitch to the left.

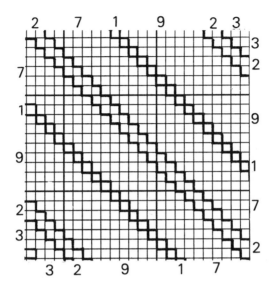

Diagram 29. Diagonal stripe, left-directed, symmetrical

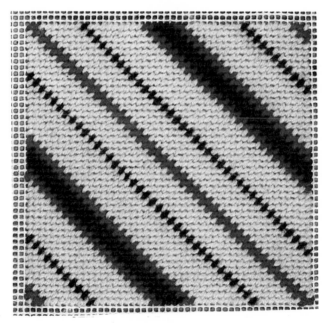

Symmetrical diagonal stripe, left-directed.

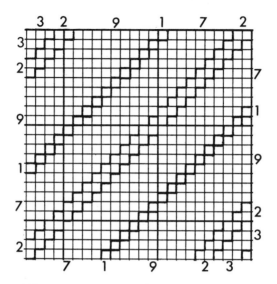

Diagram 30. Diagonal stripe, right-directed, symmetrical

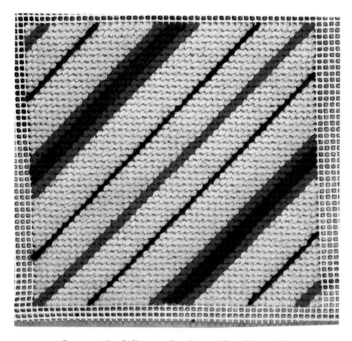

Symmetrical diagonal stripe, right-directed.

Symmetrical left-directed diagonal stripe used as a background for the All-Over Initial pattern on a Baxwood lamp. The stripe was based on the date March 10 1950. Notice that 10 rows were used to replace the zero after the 5 in the year. The letter on the lamp is from the DMC alphabet on pages 34–36. The letter holder was made in a matching stripe on 7-to-the-inch plastic canvas, finished and photographed by Rhoda Goldberg.

DIAGONAL PLAID

Combining the diagonal stripes of both directions to form a diagonal (argyle) plaid, the every-other-basketweave stitch is used to provide spaces for the two angles to meet. Stitching from lower right to upper left, use the basketweave stitch for one "up" row. Then skip one stitch to the left of your last stitch at the top and start your "down" row. When you reach the bottom, skip one stitch to the left and start another "up" row. This can be continued for as many rows of one color as you have in your birth-date pattern. When doing a diagonal plaid, be sure you *count only the stitched rows* when counting in your number pattern, even though you are skipping rows between them.

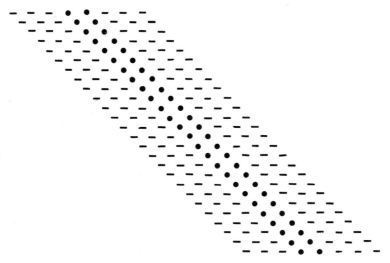

Diagram 31.   Step 1: diagonal plaid, lower right to upper left stitches

Diagram 32.   Step 2: diagonal plaid, upper right to lower left stitches

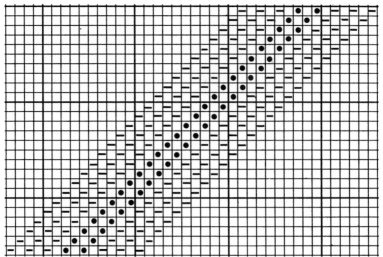

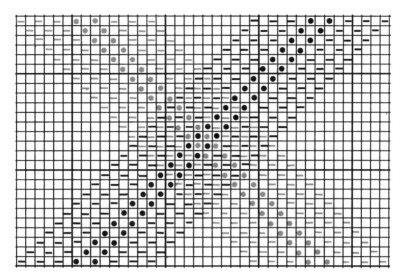

Diagram 33.   Combined diagonal plaid stitches

Symmetrical diagonal plaid.

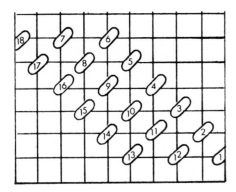

Diagram 34. Basketweave stitch sequence: every other row, lower right to upper left

Diagram 35. Basketweave stitch sequence every other row, upper right to lower left

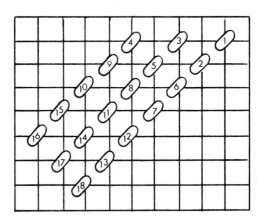

Symmetrical diagonal plaid checkbook cover inspired by a man's sport jacket. The five-color pattern is: (center) 8A, 8B, 4C, 2D, 4C, 4E, then repeat from 8A.

Symmetrical diagonal plaid pillow with three changing color patterns, based on the date February 7, 1923.

Diagonal plaid executed on 14 mesh canvas based on the date May 3, 1915. The textured effect is the result of using DMC embroidery cotton, perle cotton and Persian yarn in adjacent sections. The Accent telephone from the Design Line of the New York Telephone Company was used with their permission.

Magazine rack sling in a symmetrical diagonal plaid based on the date July 5, 1919. The border is a stripe in the same number pattern.

Complete all your rows from lower right to upper left first. Then start from the upper right and work your way diagonally to the lower left, moving one row down and one stitch to the left, in the spaces left by skipping rows when you were working from lower right to upper left. You will see that where stripes of the same color and width meet you will have a diamond shape. Where stripes of the same color and different widths meet you will have a rectangular shape. As you experiment with colors and widths of stripes, you may discover interesting shapes appearing, surprising you as you stitch! If you don't want to be surprised, work out your pattern on graph paper first.

STRAIGHT PLAID, SYMMETRICAL

The straight plaid is achieved by stitching every other square of mesh with a diagonal stitch (tent, half-cross, or basketweave), both horizontally and vertically. The stitching may be done one row at a time using the half-cross or tent stitch, or several rows at a time using the every-other-basketweave stitch.

In the basic example, every other stitch was done in red for two rows in the center horizontally, then for two rows in the center vertically. On either side of these center ("month") rows, the "day" rows were stitched (7 rows white). Next to that the "year" rows were stitched: 1 row of red, 9 rows of white, 2 rows of red, and 3 rows of blue. This is the basic symmetrical straight plaid.

Diagram 36.   Every other stitch: one row horizontal, one row vertical

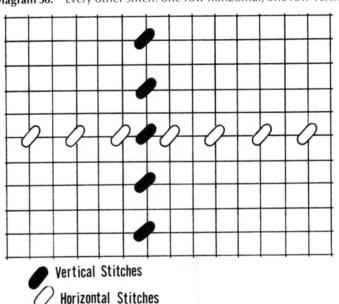

⬤ **Vertical Stitches**

⬤ **Horizontal Stitches**

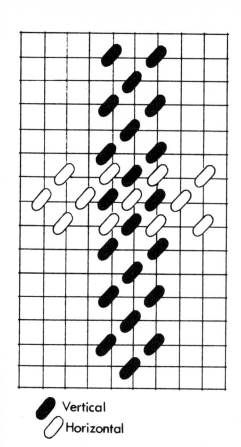

Vertical

Horizontal

Diagram 37.   Three vertical and three horizontal rows

Diagram 38.   Symmetrical straight plaid using the date February 7, 1923

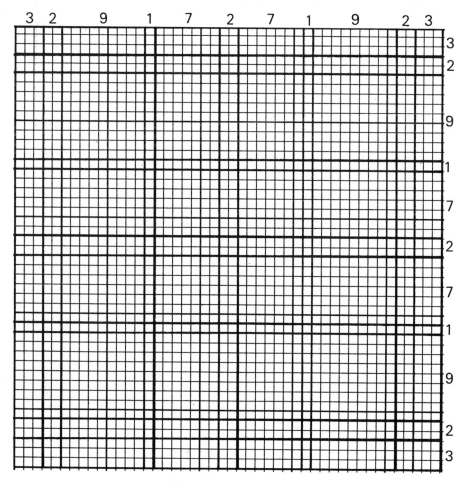

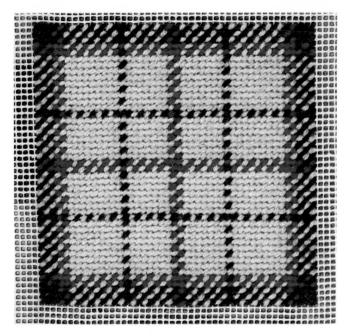

Symmetrical straight plaid.

Footstool cover design based on the date April 12, 1912, executed by Lois Nalevaiko of Port Jefferson, N.Y.

Symmetrical straight plaid design on a tennis racquet cover made by Jack Shaffer of Huntington, N.Y. All the vertical rows have been done and the horizontal rows have been started. This was a very ambitious undertaking for one who had never needlepointed before!

Pocketbook design based on the date December 15, 1948, made by Mrs. Alfred Levy of Huntington, N.Y.

Celebrating our country's bicentennial, Jacqui Goldberg, aged 12, made this straight plaid pillow using the numbers 1776–1976.

STRAIGHT PLAID, REPEATING

The repeating straight plaid starts with the basic color pattern, but continues with variations in color. To change the colors in the second repeat, we let A = white, B = blue, and C = red. The number pattern remains the same, but the color pattern is now

white	A
blue	B
red	C
blue	B
white	A
red	C

The third variation is A = blue, B = red, and C = white.

blue	A
red	B
white	C
red	B
blue	A
white	C

Repeating straight plaid with three changing color patterns.

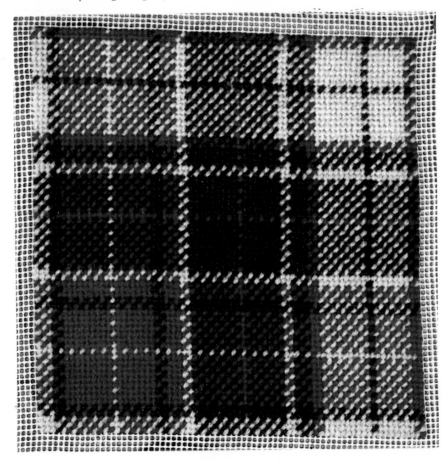

Repeating straight plaid pillow based on the date August 7, 1951.

When making a larger piece, you would repeat the number pattern again using the *first* color pattern. If you are making up your own repeating color pattern, be sure that the last color of a pattern is different from the first color of the next variation. If not, the last and first sections will blend together and the number pattern will be lost.

The same series of repeating color patterns was used in the horizontal and vertical repeating stripes and in the diagonal plaid pillow.

Repeating horizontal and vertical stripes with three changing color patterns.

DESIGNING YOUR OWN PATTERN

To make it easier for you to start experimenting immediately, we have included several pages of graph paper at the back of the book, in both 10-squares-to-the-inch and 12-squares-to-the-inch. You can use colored felt-tip markers in each square to denote a thread color, or you can use a symbol such as a dot, dash, slash, or plus sign. If you do use symbols, be sure to write the legend to indicate the colors they stand for (for example, / = red, + = blue, etc.). Then it will be easy to follow when you start to stitch. When you have a pattern that suits you, it's simple to translate it to canvas with your needle and yarn, since every square on the graph paper is equal to one stitch on the canvas.

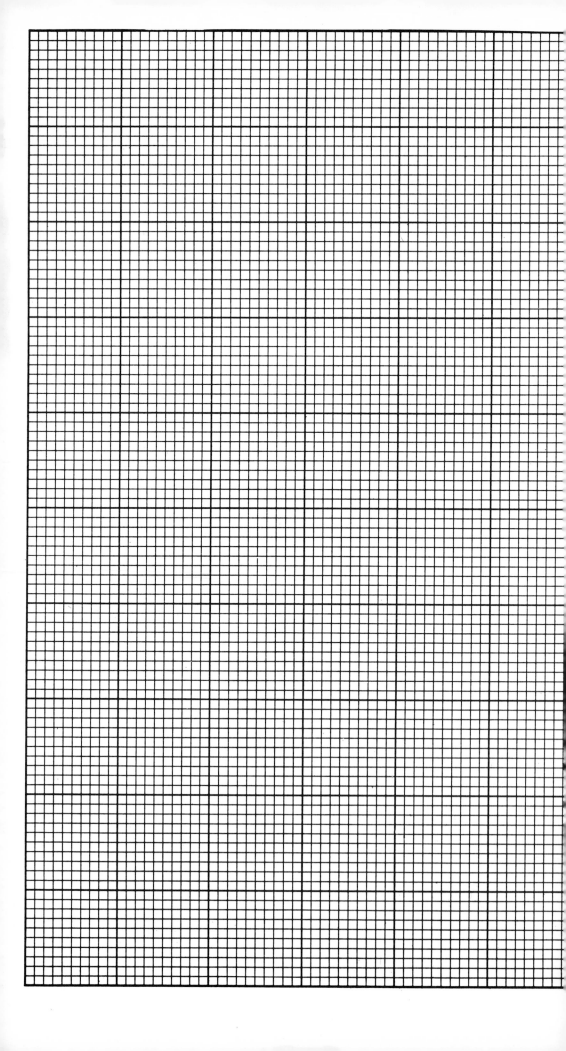

Supply Sources

DMC Corporation
107 Trumbull St.
Elizabeth, N.J. 07206

DMC Library of Letters,
Floralia Persian yarn,
embroidery floss

The New York Telephone Co.

Accent telephone

Craft Accessories
615 Linwood Drive
Midland, Mich. 48640

Baxwood lamp, Dazor
magnifying lamp

Amaro & Sons
4888 Ronson Court
San Diego, Calif. 92111

Luggage rack, embroidery
hoops and stands

Eagle Buckram Co., Inc.
29 West 4th St.
New York, N.Y. 10012

Magazine rack, tennis
racquet cover, tennis
visor

Modern Needlepoint Mounting
Co.
11 West 32nd St.
New York, N.Y. 10001

Handbags, phone book covers,
belts, eyeglass cases,
bell pulls

Eleanor Frank
61 Scholar Lane
Commack, N.Y. 11725

Pillow finishing

Carl Adler
26 Glenwood Rd.
Glen Head, N.Y. 11545

Upholstery

Needlegraph
Box 186
Dix Hills, N.Y. 11746

Black-lined graph paper 10, 12, and
14 squares to the inch, for design
charting, reproducible

Index